A Poem For Faith

I Was An Atheist Till I Saw Her.....

Oh Shit I Still Am One.....

Currently The Only Thing I Have Faith In

Is My Lesbian Tendencies & Suicidal Ones.....

Faith Is So Gorgeous....

With Her Teased Feathered Amber Hair...

& Perfect Eyebrows...

& Soft Fair Skin.....

Even Her Sadness Is Beautiful....

With Her Long Dainty Cut Up Legs...

She's A Psychiatric Princess...

She Gives Me The Jitters

Cause She The Sexiest Of All The Wrist-Slitters

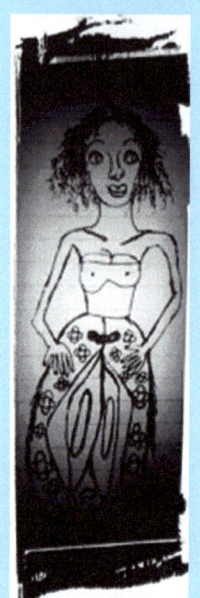

I Love Her.....

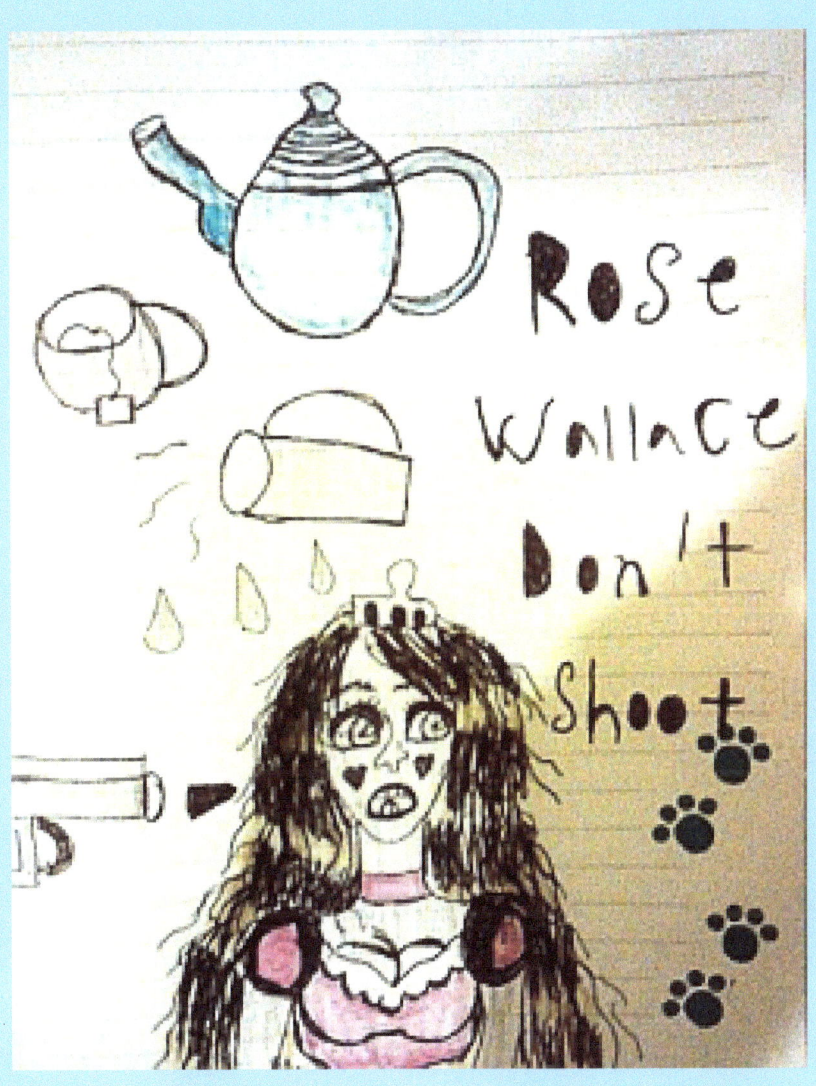

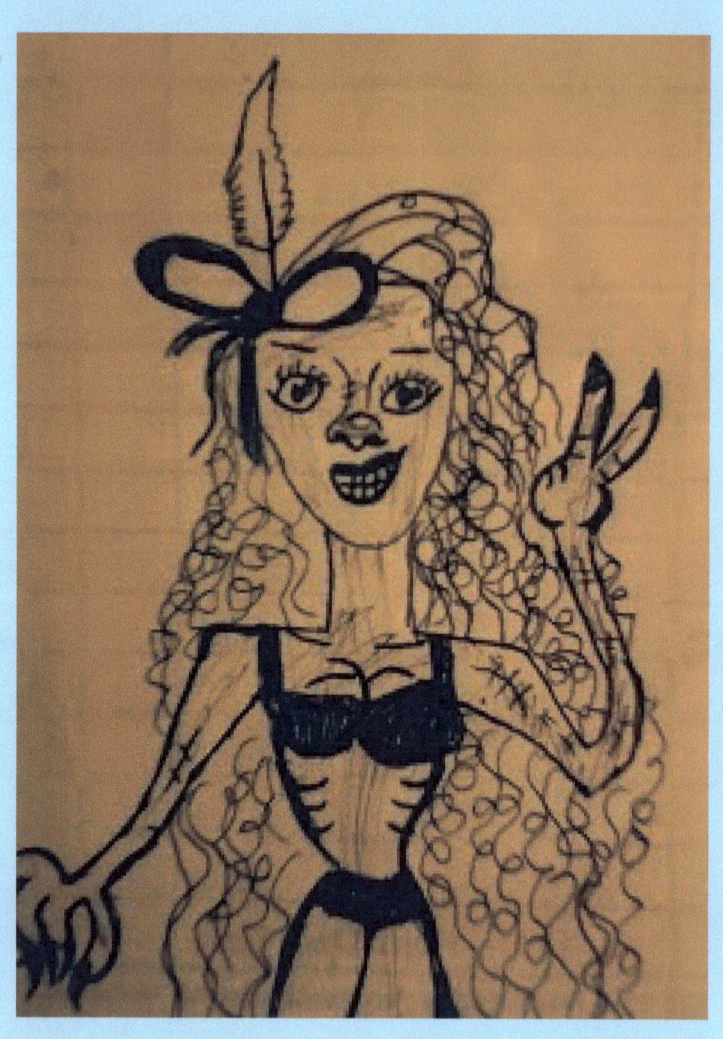

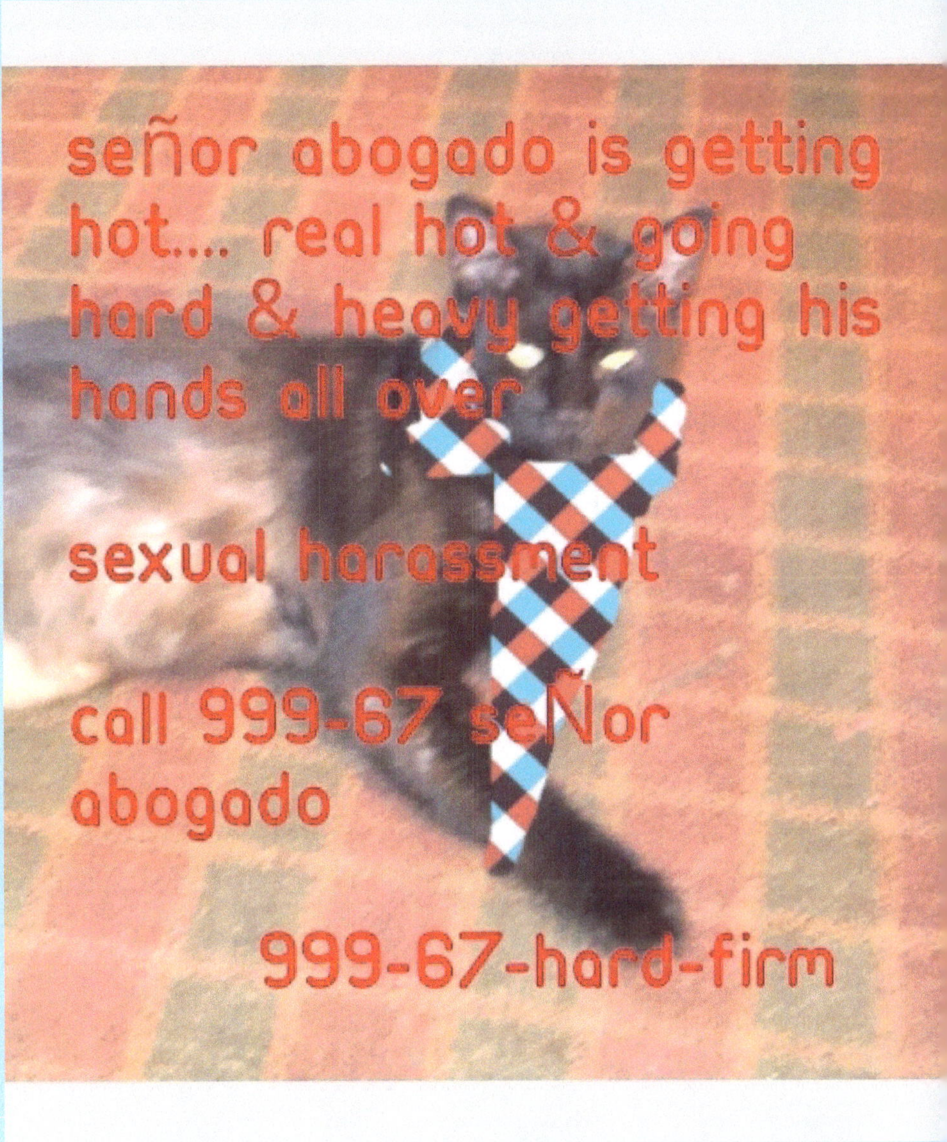

señor abogado is getting hot.... real hot & going hard & heavy getting his hands all over

sexual harassment

call 999-67 seÑor abogado

999-67-hard-firm

Angel Dust Abandonment

Angel Dust Abandonment Lonely Lone Wolf Guzzling Lone Star Beer Heating Up A Stolen Can Of 70¢ Chili Outside A Chili's Cause He's Too Poor To Eat At Chili's & He Tried To Get A Job At Chili's But They Don't Like Hobos & All The Neighborhood Kids Give Him Wet-Willies & His Momma Said He Looked Like Willy Nelson Before She Died Of Syphilis Her Name Was Philis Phillips He's Just One Of The Forlorn Pill-Billies Stoned Again With The Dr.Phill Sillies Feeling Feelings Felt It When You Felt Me Up Sexual Violation No Translation Anorexic Transgender No Trans-Fat Transcending The Pain Tweedle-Dee Tweedle-Dum I Need A Needle & Some Heroin Selfish Mother Allergic To Shell-Fish Shoving Me In A Psych-Ward Which Is Were I Wrote This Cause I Was Very Bored

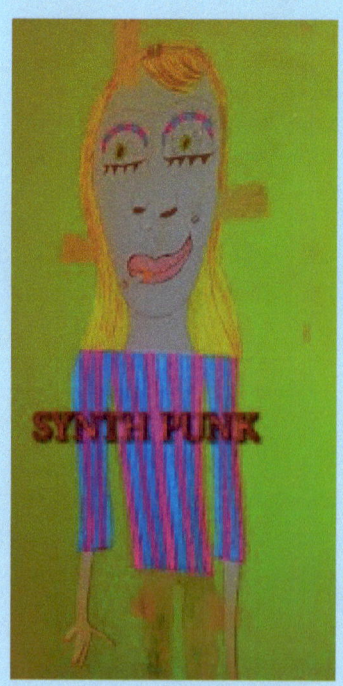

Blondie Depp Again

IF ONLY MY WEIGHT WAS AS LOW AS MY IQ FUCK YOU MAN YOU DIDNT JUST LEAD ME ON YOU LED ME TO KILL MYSELF YOU SHOWED ME LOVE YOU SHOWED ME BEAUTY & TOOK IT AWAY LIKE IT'S SOME KINDA TOY & I'M A CHILD WHO'S IN TROUBLE FOR DRAWING ON THE WALL MY GHOST IS WRITING THIS CAUSE ILL NEED YOU FOREVER I MISS YOU COME BACK IF YOU DONT COME BACK IM GOING TO TRAP YOUR SOUL IN MY WITCHES JAR & TAKE YOU OUT ONLY AT NIGHT WHEN IM LONELY LUSTING & LONGING FOR A MAN IF I WASNT SO DAMN HIGH YOUR LACK OF RESPONSE WOULD'VE MADE ME CRY!!!

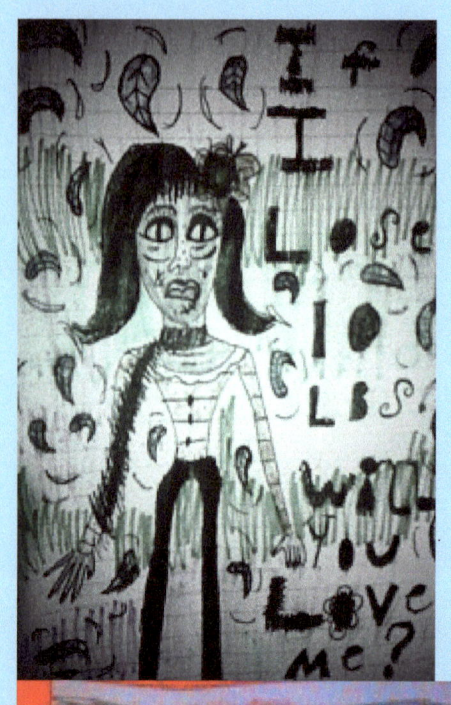
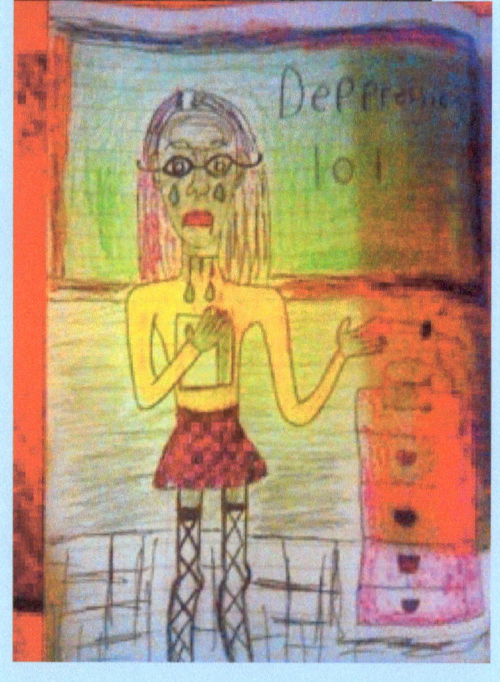

Blondie Depp

Blonde Johnny Depp He's So Perfect He Doesn't Even Know He's Perfect Which Makes Him Even More Perfect Peroxide To Hide The Darkness Inside Have I Died? Have I Died? & Gone To Heaven! He's Too Good For Me! & Too Far Away!! But Id I'd Go All The Way To Florida To Go All The Way With Him!!

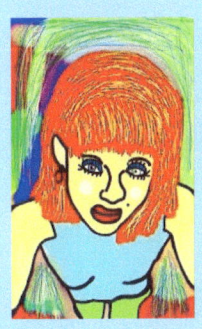

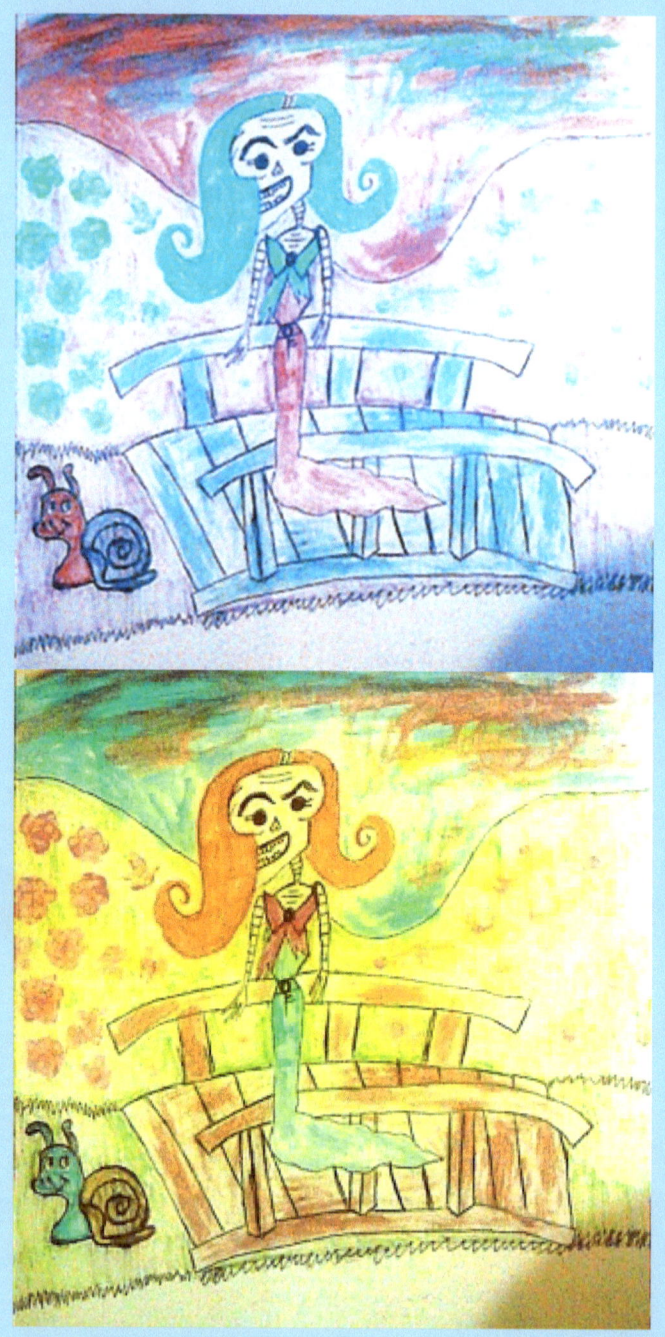

COCAINE COMPASSION

Cocaine compassion & Wrist Slashing & Meth Head Facial Mashing & Its 2 AM & Then It'll Be 3 AM & Sleep Becomes More & More Elusive & Paranoia Drives Me To Be Reclusive & The River Splits & My Mouth Chews & Spits & I Have mad Ex-Lax Shits & You'll Find Me Crying To The Greatest Hits Of The Smiths & Avoiding My Scheduled Shifts & It Rifts & Rifts Endlessly Mindlessly Dully Another Day Blending Smearing Like Cheap Paints Into Another Night No More Cocaine Compassion Forever Crashing Don't Wake Me Don't Startle Don't Stare Don't Speak No More Cocaine Compassion Just Forever Crashing

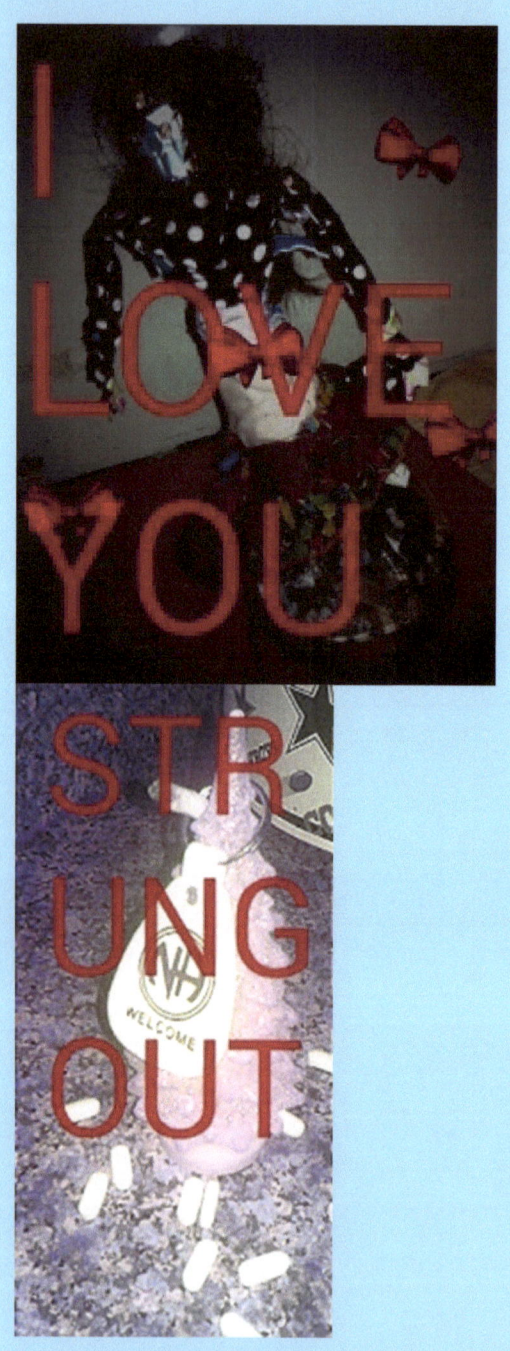

Dear Suzie

Suzie. I Broke Into Your House & Roofied You & Fucked You While You Were Passed Out Because You Said In Your Diary You Were Lonely For A Man & You Just Want Someone To Make You Laugh & Smile Here's A Joke: Knock Knock Who's There? Yo Dead Mamma! LOL XOXOX You Also Said You Were Ready To Have Babies So I Replaced Your Birth Control With Pink Xanaxes A Week A Go Sorry About The Whole Losing Your Job As A Janitor At The Strip Club Cause You Passed Out On A Semen Covered Urinal Suzie I Also Drank All Your Beer To Save You From Yourself Cause I Think You Have A Serious Problem With Alcohol Those Pecan Pies You Took Hours To Make Were The Shit I Ate All 15 Of Them Cause You're Getting Fat & I Didn't Clean Up The Puke Cause You Could Use Some Exercise Cleaning My Barf Trail From The Kitchen To The Top Of Your Stairs I Did However Take The Liberty Of Burning Your 100 Year Old Quilt Passed Down From Generation To Generation Cause I'm A Gentleman & I Also Threw Up On It Anyways Suzie I Just Wanted You To

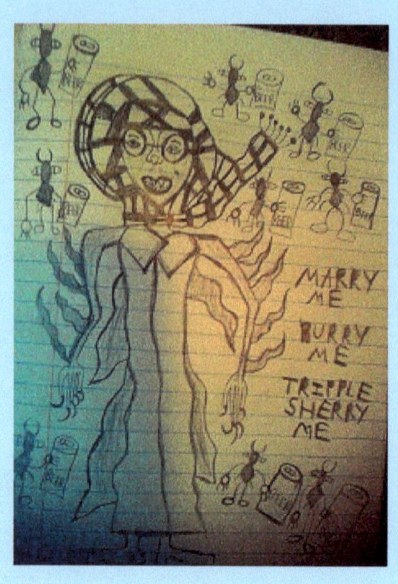

Dharma/Dahmer

Have You Ever Felt A Lust You Couldn't Satisfy? Are You Hankering For A New Exotic Taste? Jeffrey Was Lost Just Like You Once. Learn His Wisdom

Definition Of Dharma:

1. essential quality or character, as of the cosmos or one's own nature.

2. conformity to one's own quality or character.

3. virtue manly strength, courage and a capacity to act

4. religion is a personal set of attitudes, and practices

Jeffrey Lionel Dahmer, a son, a friendly neighbor a Miller beer enthusiast and a loyal McDonald's customer. He lowered his carbon foot print by walking and using public transportation. Jeffrey, also known as the Milwaukee Cannibal, was an American serial killer and sex offender, who committed the rape, murder, and dismemberment of seventeen men and boys between 1978 and 1991

Are you edible?

Are you bedible?

Are you edible and bedible?

Yes.

Yes.

Yes and yes.

For you, the answer is regrettable.

Their is no Noble Scientific proof that Buddhism can lead to Cannibalism or that they are anyway related, other than the spiritual truth taught by Nirvanas spokesman All in All is All we are. Their is also no such thing as Nobel Science and more than likely no spiritual truth .

Embarrassment

I PUT THE BAR IN EMBARRASSMENT WHEN I POP A HANDLEBAR I PUT THE ASS IN EMBARRASSMENT EVERYDAY I PUT THE MEANT IN EMBARRASSMENT CAUSE I MEAN EVERY DUMB THING I FUCKING SAY I PUT THE E MINOR IN EMBARRASSMENT ALL THOSE NUDES I FORGOT I SENT GOD I CANT REPENT THERE'S A DENT IN MY BRAIN QUICK!!!! GET ME A PAIN PILL SO I CAN DEAL WITH ALL THIS EMBARRASSMENT I FEEL!!! I'M ABASHED! PLEASE! SOMEONE! BASH MY HEAD IN! I'M SLIGHTLY HUMILIATED BY ALL THE DRUNK SEX I'VE PARTICIPATED IN.... GRACE? LOVE? INNER-BEAUTY? I GUESS IT IT PRETTY BEAUTIFUL WHEN HE IS IN ME....WHEN THE SYRINGE IS IN ME

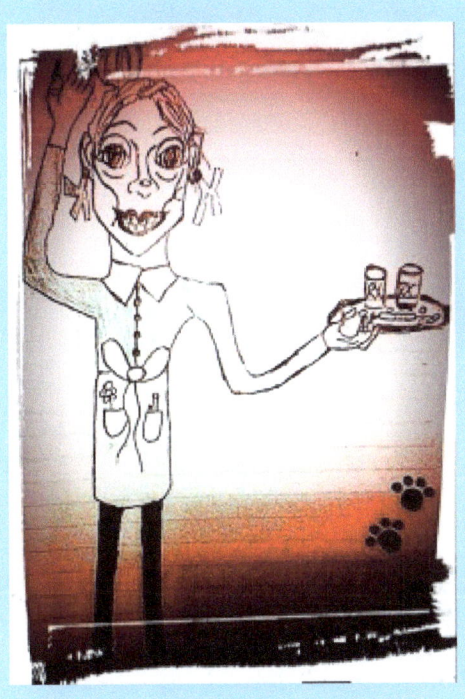

Fuck Cops

FUCK THE COPS IT'S BEEN SAID A BILLION TIMES BUT HASN'T BEEN SAID ENOUGH FUCK COPS RIGHT UP THEIR TUGHT SMELLY PUCKERED ASSHOLES WITH SPIKED DILDOS THEY ARE JUST GAY SADOMASOCHIST WITH THEIR CUFFS CLUBS & S & M UNIFORMS DON'T JUST FUCK THEM RAPE & KILL THEM TEACH EM A LESSON FOR LOCKING ME UP & STEALING MY METH & HEROIN THAT I EARNED FROM AN HONEST HARD DAYS WORK SUCKING COCK AT THE TRUCK STOP TILL MY JAW FELT LIKE IT WAS GONNA FALL OFF FUCK COPS!!!

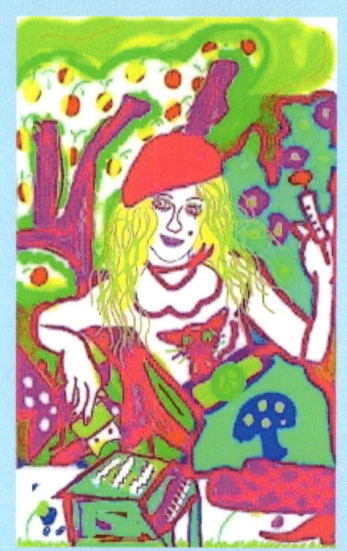

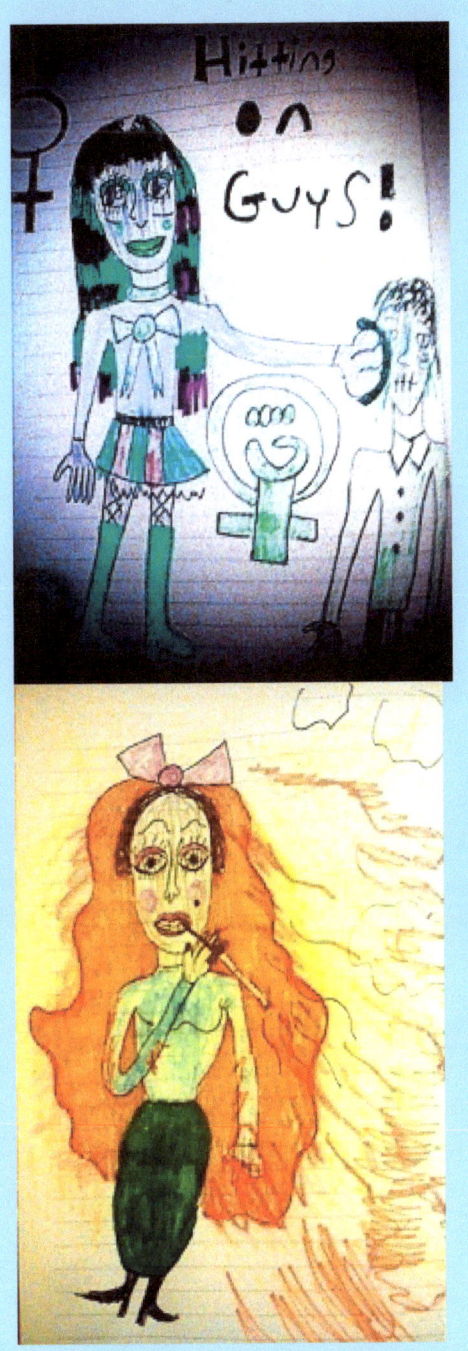

HAVE AN AFFAIR WITH A MERMAID

Q. What do you call a mermaid housekeeper?

A. A mer-MAID

Q. What kinda men eat mermaids out when they are on their periods?

A. Sharks

Q. How did Maria Dariah The Mermaid Make A Margarita While Bartending At The #1 gay bar in the Pacific ocean?

A. She Mermaid It?

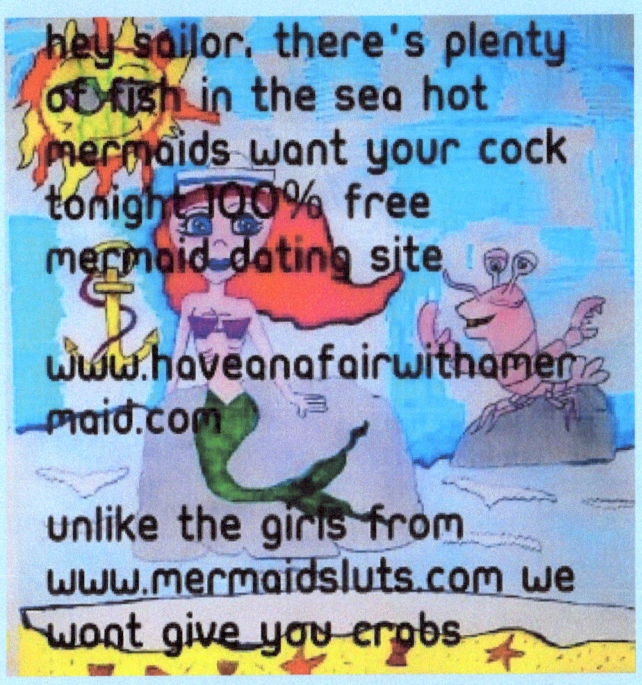

Heroin, Acid, Meth, Shrooms, Miscellaneous

I Met A Schizophrenic Lady Named Tanya Who Was Not Your Typical Psychiatric Geriatric... She Thought I Was Her Daughter Christina & Kept Hugging Me & Saying, "I Love You." I Went Along With It...She Seemed To Love Me More Than My Actual Mom.... She Kept Yelling "I Have A Snake In My Vagina." I Spent A Day With Her At A Holding Unit...We Watched TV & She Thought They Were Airing Live Footage Of Her Son Being Decapitated...She Also Believed The Hospital Staff Was Conspiring To Kill Her & Continuously

Requested For The Doctors To Remove The Snake In Her Vagina & Was Furious That They Wouldn't......

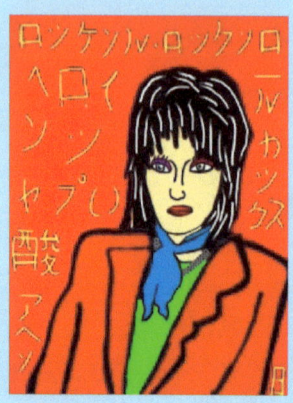

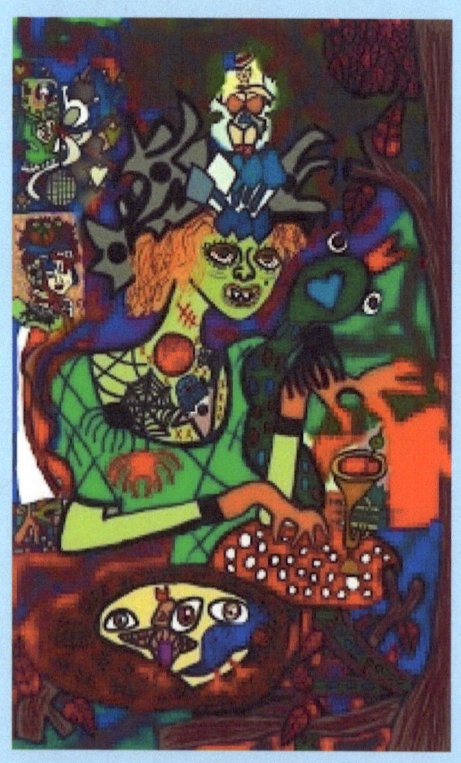

WORDS OF WISDOM: Being A Man/Getting The Job Done

It's all about standing by your decisions & finishing what you started...In Other Words If You Click On Some Really Gross Porn Just Keep Going Anyway 'Till You Cum

Heroin, Acid, Meth, Shrooms, Miscellaneous

I Met A Schizophrenic Lady Named Tanya Who Was Not Your Typical Psychiatric Geriatric... She Thought I Was Her Daughter Christina & Kept Hugging Me & Saying, "I Love You." I Went Along With It...She Seemed To Love Me More Than My Actual Mom.... She Kept Yelling "I Have A Snake In My Vagina." I Spent A Day With Her At A Holding Unit...We Watched TV & She Thought They Were Airing Live Footage Of Her Son Being Decapitated...She Also Believed The Hospital Staff Was Conspiring To Kill Her & Continuously Requested For The Doctors To Remove The Snake In Her Vagina & Was Furious That They Wouldn't......

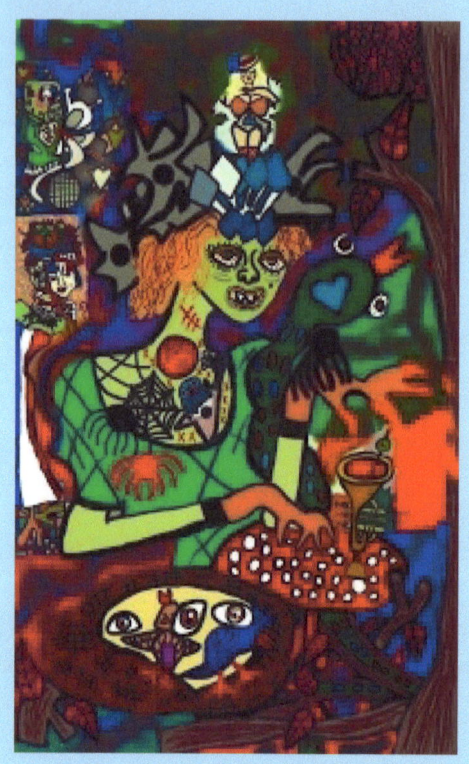

HOT NEW CLUB LA NASTY DICK

Jeffry Dahmer & Norman Bates Walk Into A Black Gay Bar Called La Nasty Dick

Jeffrey Dahmer Orders A Cocktail & Says "I Like My Rum Like I Like My Men Cold, Dark, & Fruity"

He Turns To Norman Bates & Ask "Do You Come Here Often?"

Norman Bates Replies "No I NORMA-lly Don't. I'm Heterosexual"

Jeffrey Dahmer Says, "Heterosexual? More Like Hetero-Digestible I Could Just Eat You Up Cutie. It's Been Years Since I Had Hot Lean White Meat In A Snack."

Norman Bates Goes, "Hell No You Ain't Gonna Fry My Juicy Bits Bitch!"

Then Jeffrey Dahmer Says, "You Misheard Me. I Said In The Sack! I Wanna Bang You Like A Gong! I Want You To Be My Sexy Little Normandy Bomb! I Want You To Make My Dick Explode With Pleasure!"

Norman Bates Was Pissed So He Pulled Out A Shiv & Yelled, "Back The Fuck Up, It's Like My Momma Norma Always Say Norman Will Shank A Nigger If He's Gots-Ta!"

Jeffrey Dahmer Says, "Whatevs You Creepy Motherfucker You Must Be Psycho Or Some Shit? I Ain't Scared, You're Just A God Damned Pussy Mommas Boy! Wtf Was Your Name Again Punk!? Mormon Masturbates! GTFO!!!!"

Then The Bartender Interrupts & Ask For Them To Pay

Norman Bates Is All Like, "Fuck Man! This Is Gonna Cost Me An Arm & A Leg! My Mom Said I Could Have One Big Boy Drink But I Had To Buy Her Lube & New Batteries For Her Dildo With The Rest Of The Money!"

Jeffrey Dahmer Pulls A Black Arm & Leg Out Of His Tote Bag & Tips The Bartender With A Big Black Cock.

Norman Bates Says, "Thanks Man I Owe You! Feel Free To Come Over Anytime & But Fuck Me Bro!"

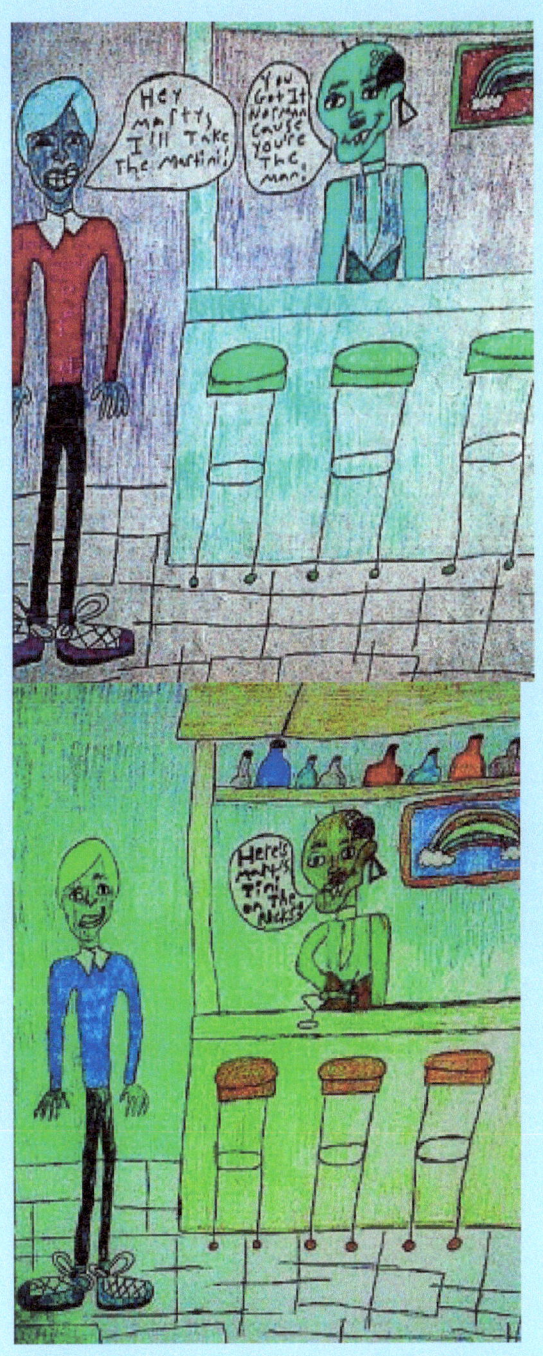

I Died

I Am A Dead Body I Am Always Cold That's Why I'll Get In Bed With Anybody Who Will Have Me To Try & Warm Up To Try & Feel Less Alone It's Lonely Being A Corpse I Used To Have A Heart But Now I'm Just A Crude Parody Of The Girl I Used To Be & I've Been Having Nightmares About Lesbian Hookers Infecting Me With Aids & I Just Don't Know Anymore

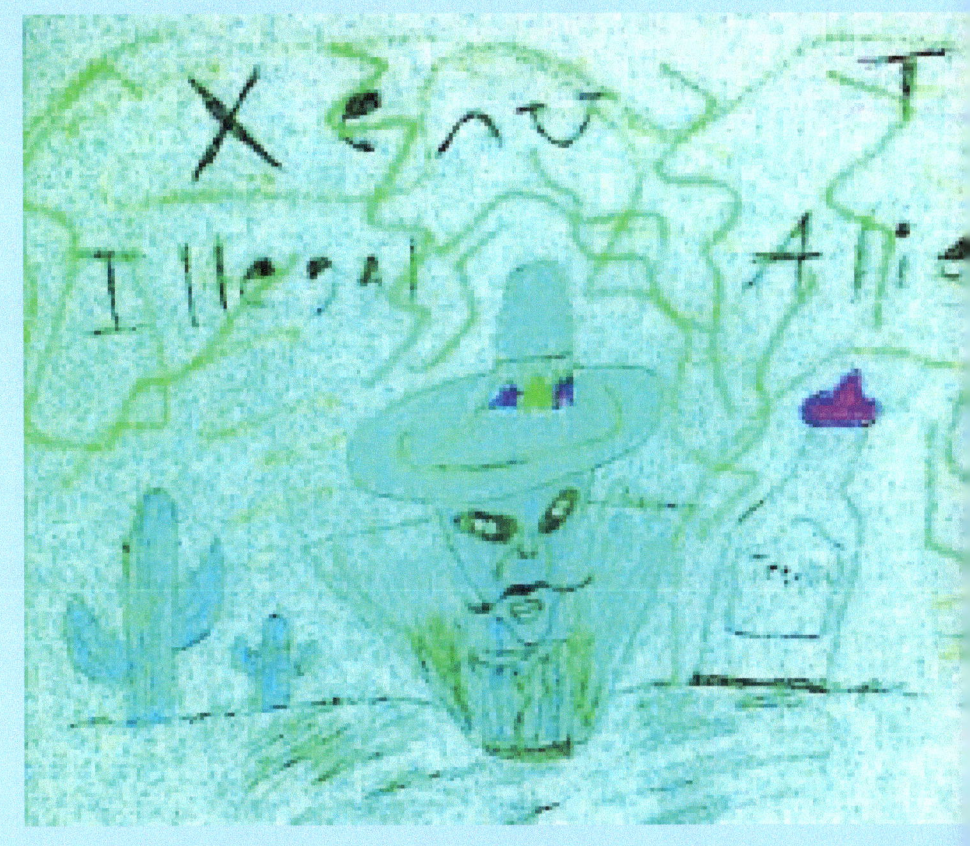

I QUOTE MYSELF

-I Take Lithium Cause I'm A Bisexual Polar Bear

-I Used My Therapist Tits As Stress Balls & Now I'm In Legal Trouble

-You Got To Know Your Audience…..Mine Is Anyone Stuck Listening

-I Feel A Great Sense Of Belonging At The Psych Ward

-Where Can I Buy A Nice Cozy Tempurpedic Deathbed On A Strippers' Salary?

-Let's Get The Old Gang Bang Back Together…

-Do You Like Seafood!? Good! Cause I Got Crabs!!!

-Does My Bulimia Make You Nervosa? Take A Xanax…

-Why Did I Get Fired For Nodding On The Toilet At Work?! It's Called A Rest Room!!!

-Silent But Deadly Farts Have Social Anxiety…. That's Why They're So Quiet…..

-I Am A Serious Writer… Of Erotic Fan-Fiction, Suicide Notes, & Grocery List That Read Vodka & Potatoes Chips

-I'm So Excited & I Just Can't Hide It... Seriously Someone Help.... Get Me Some Tape

-The Only Thing More Useless Than You Is Non-Alcoholic Beer...

-There's No Such Thing As A Tough Pill To Swallow... I Love Pills

-My Chronic Depression Isn't Just A Passing Case Of The Blues....It's A Case Of The Reggae's

-I Do, Do Drugs.... I Shit You Not

-I Honestly Need To Get Better At Lying

-An Orgasm A Day Keeps The Doctor Away....

-Workaholics Anonymous.... It Works If You Don't Work It....

-Ask A Queer What An 8-Ball Is & He'll Tell You It's 4 Guys.....

-She Said I Came On Too Strong... That Must Mean She Thinks I'm A Sexy Muscle Man....That's The Only Thing It Could Mean....

-When Nappy Hair Turns A Chick On....It'S Called An Afro-Disiac

-Codeine Makes A Great Pancake Syrup....You're Welcome

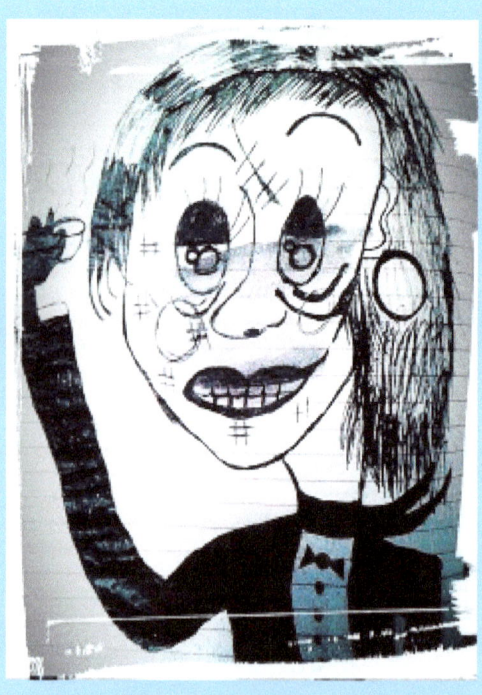

I'm Repulsive Check My Pulse I May Have Overdosed

I'm an alcoholic in love with a bartender.....

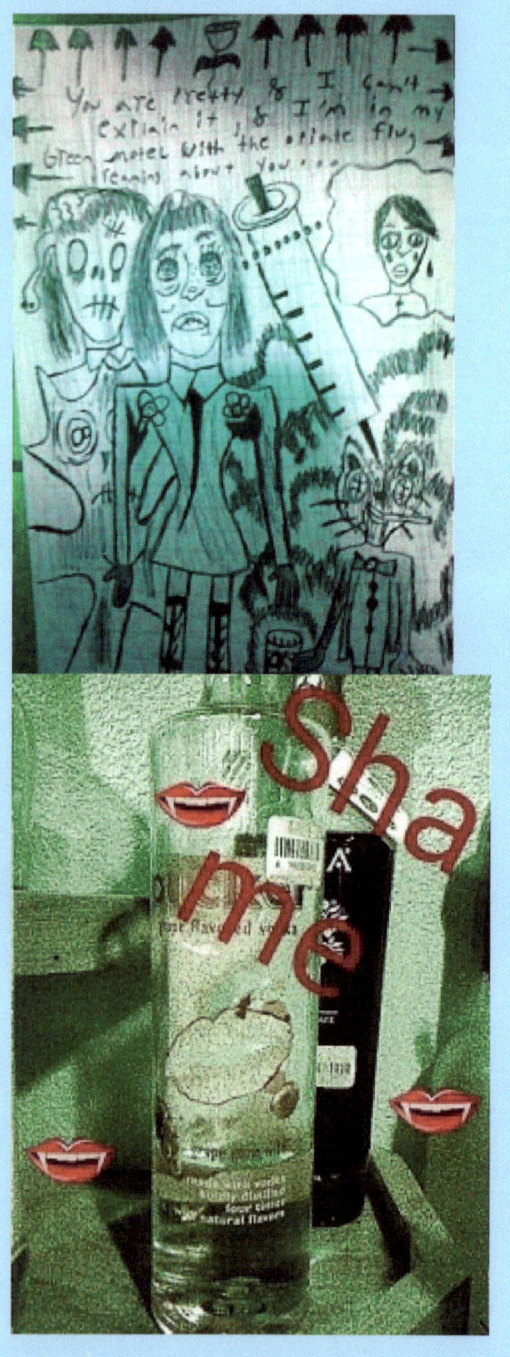

I'M ENGAGED

My Pillow Loves Me More
Than Any Man Can
Canned Cat Food Smells
& We Suffer Isolated In Our
Inner Shells Were It's Safe
I'm So Alone I Masturbate
'Till I Chafe I'm Going To
Purge Until I'm A Waif
Puking Vanilla Wafers But
At Least My Pillow Loves
Me Unconditionally & He'd
Never Judge Me So I
Guess I Can't Complain

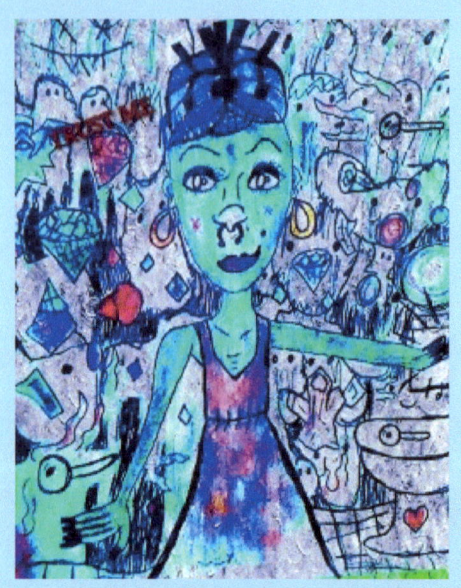

Looking For Soul Food & A Place To Eat

Jeffy Deez Diner Ended Racism By Being The First Restaurant To Serve Blacks

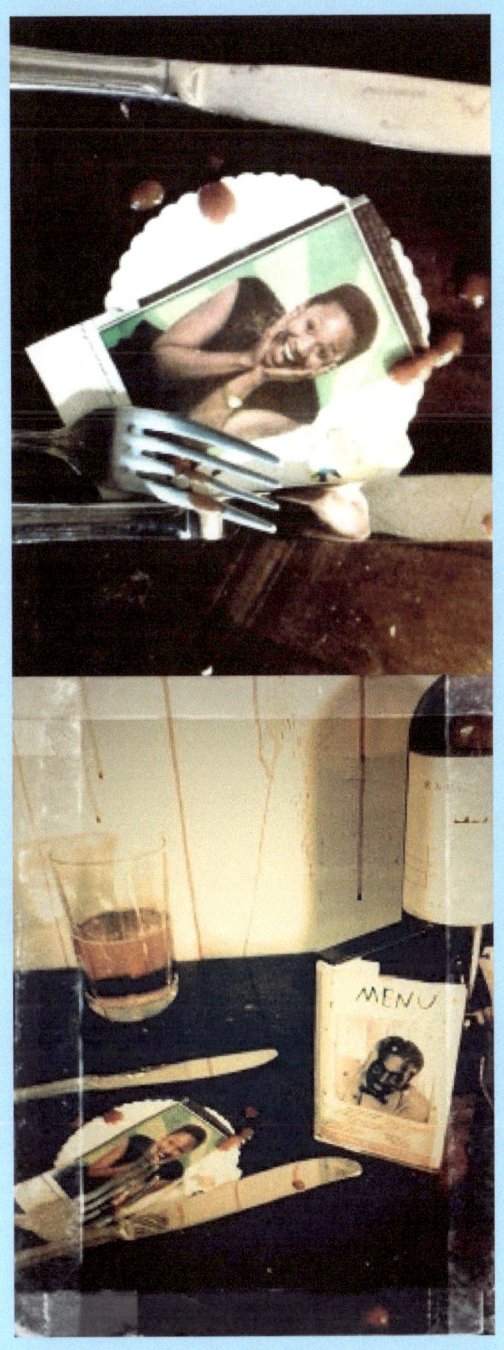

MENTAL LINTEL!!!

Even My Imaginary Friends Hate Me....That's How Much I Suck, Why Does My Therapist Say I Have "Abandonment Issues", When The MotherFucking Truth Is That Everything I Love Leaves...Even My Alcohol & Pills Leave Me... I Let Them In My Mouth & Then They Are Gone.... Just Like Men... I'm Stuck Alone...SOBER, SOMBER, SAD, & SUICIDALLY SLUTTY.... My Therapist Keeps A File In Her Desk Documenting All Of My Personal Failures & Mental Defects...... I'm Not A Pinto Bean.... I'm Not Even A Fucking Black-Eye Pea.... I'm The Worst Food Of All....... A MENTAL LINTEL

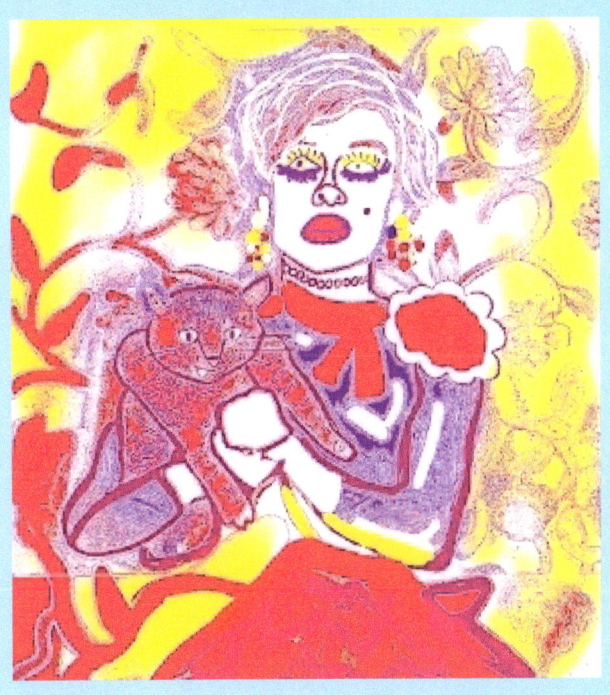

MY LOVE

My Love Is A Prison You Can't Escape & Honey The Bars Are Made Of Xanax & I'll Strap You In The Electric Chair & Fuck You So Hard You'll Wish You Were Dead & Haven't You Heard? Crazy Girls Give The Best Head & Trust Me You'll Get Off But You're Not Getting Off Easy I Got You Pinned Down In Cuffs Cause My Love Is A Prison You Can't Escape

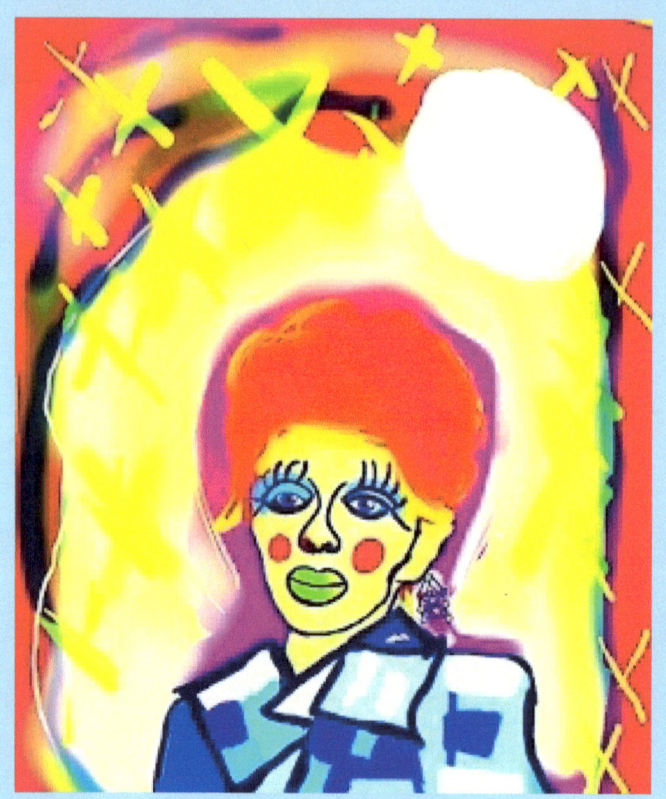

NIHLIST

The Only Point Is The One On My Knife MotherFucker I'm A Nihlist Ain't Nothing Worth While I'm Pissed Life's A Shit Pile You Get The Gist I'm A Nihlist Shy & Always Dissed When I Die I Won't Be Missed

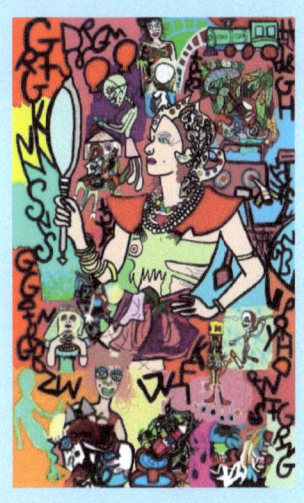

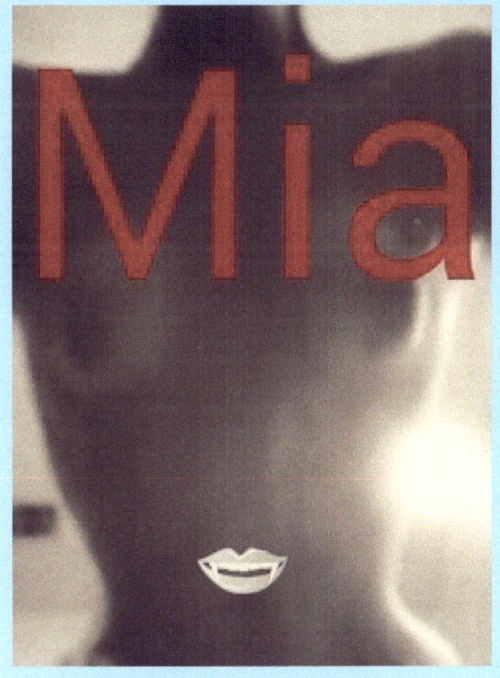

Pimp Washington

My name's George Washington I Cannot Tell A Lie Don't Ask Me Why

I be crossing them

Slave bitches with my cherry tree I'm horny as can be

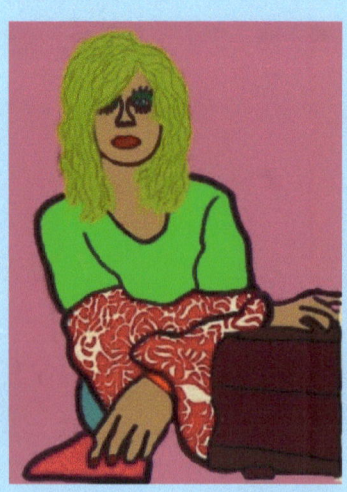

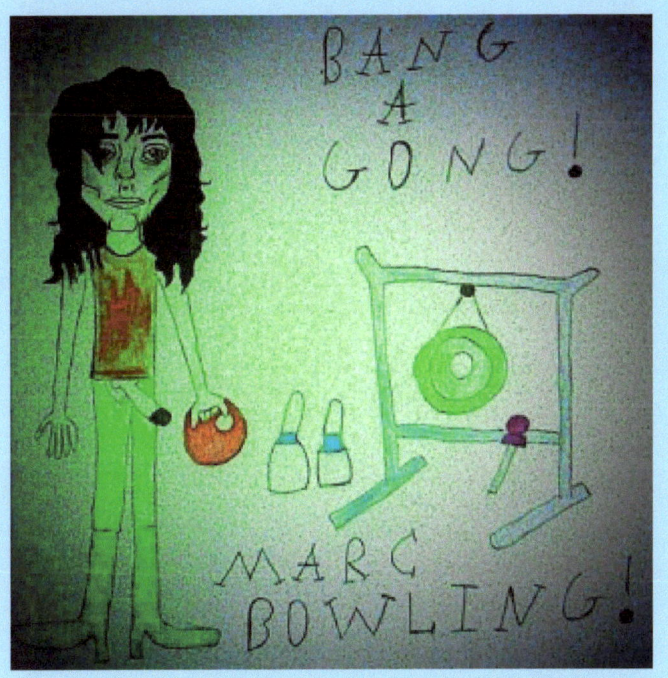

SANDRA THE MORTICIAN

Sandra Was The Mortician Of The Stars, Models, & Hollywoodlums Sandra's Job Was To Preserve The Cadaver, Re-animate It, & Install Heat/Insulation Unless The Client Wanted Stink & Coldness, Some Clients Like That Then Sandra Uses A Robotic Chip Programmed With Lines To Fulfill The Client's Fantasy Sandra's Personal Motto Is The Clients Always Right When Taylor Swift Died Her Phones Rang Off The Hooks Sandra Had To Clean & Re-Program That Cadaver More Times Than She Can Count In The Year 2045 Sandra Does This Legally In The State Of

California Thanks To The Brave Souls Who Fought Hard For Necrophile Rights Sandra Has Two Chickens & A Daughter & Loves Her Career

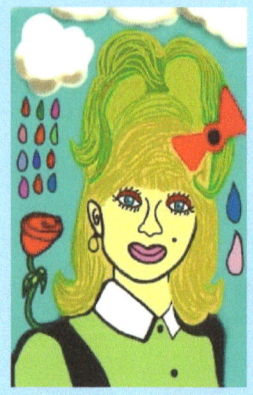

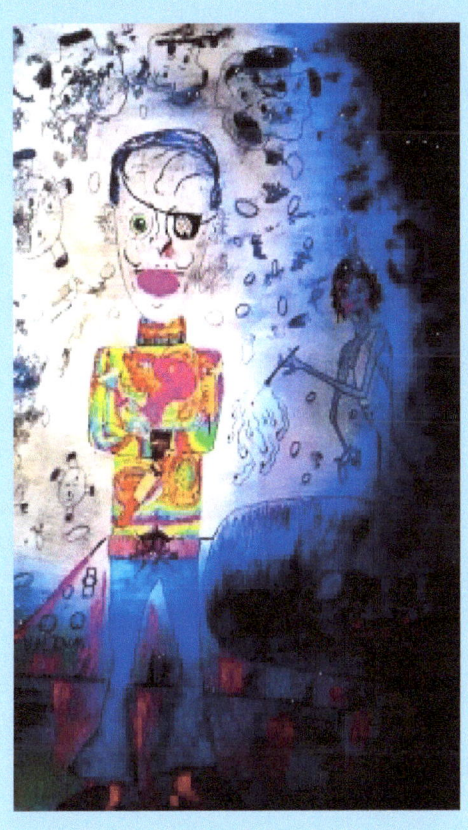

I'm Not Joking I'm Dead Fucking Serious

-Jeffrey Dahmers Not Crazy He's Just Cuckoo For Cocoa Puffs

-But Is God A Christian?

-You Know How We Can End World Hunger? By Eating My Shit!

-Girl Are You From Illinois? Cause Holy Shit Your Tittys Keep Making Lots Of Noise!

-If A Banana Is A Dick, Is A Banana Peel A Condom?

-I Asked Jeffrey Dahmer To Rollerskate. He Brought Me A Dead Prostitue Rolled Up In Carpet & Said "Why You Mad? You Told Me To Roll A Skank!"

-How Did A Stripper Become Our 1st Female President? We Liked Her On The Poles.

-Jake Was Up Against An Asian Kid During A Chest Tournament. His Name Was Mi Meeyt. Jake Won & Was So Excited From Beating That Heart-Ass Dick He Told His Mom "I Beat MI MEEYT!" "I Beat MI MEEYT!"

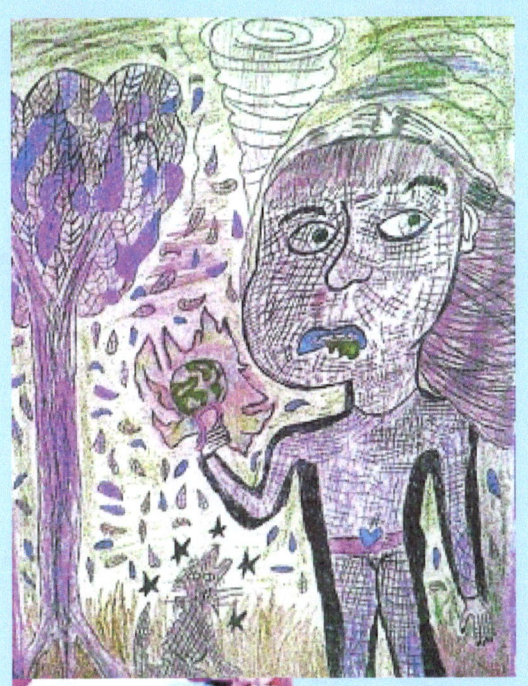
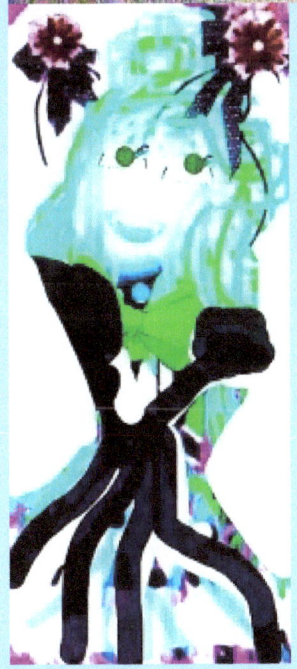

SEXUAL DAHMER-NATION

Dahmer-Nation: Is When You Sexually Dominate Someone By Killing Them & Fucking Their Dead Body

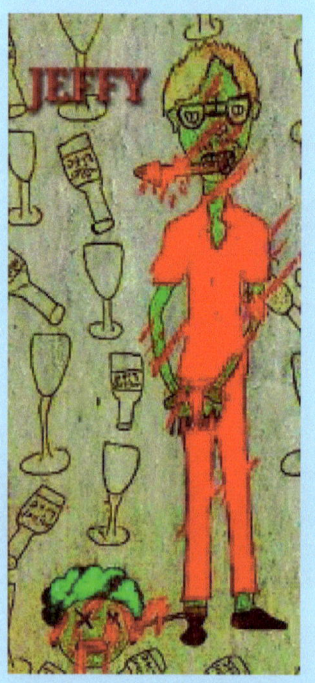

MY NAMES FRESH JEFFY D BUT YOU CAN CALL ME DAHMER CAUSE MY RHYMES GO HARDER THAN THE UNI BOMBERS WHEN IM HORNY WANTING HEAD I DECAPITATE EM ANALLY MASTERBATE EM I DO MY MEN WELL THEY BE WELL DONE CANT WAIT TO SINK MY TEETH INTO THEIR THICK BUNS JUICY BLACK MAN-WHICH HOWS A HUNGRY BOY TO RESIST IM HUNGRY LIKE THE WOLF DURAN DURAN CRACK OPEN ANOTHER CAN OF MILLER CHAMPAGNE OF BEERS TO WASH

DOWN SEXY SALTY BLACK QUEERS GONNA EAT ME ONE ON THE WAY TO MY DADS HOUSE ON THE SUBWAY IM JUST A NECROPHILIAC GAY PEACE OUT NIGGANIGGA

Smart Ass

-meningitis, bronchitis, gingivitus, hepatitis, my aunt Idis says I'm Da Illest!

-I like some Jewish boys but it's not a requirement. I just like a select few. I call those jewish guys...The chosen ones.

-Stop Playing With My Emotions & start playing with my pussy.

-My life was empty & I was going nowhere. I had no purpose I was a nihlist. Then things turned around. When I got myself some all-purpose lemon pledge.

-Hello darkness my only black friend I've come to talk with you again.

-I can't get your dick up but I can get my food up & that's what really counts in life.

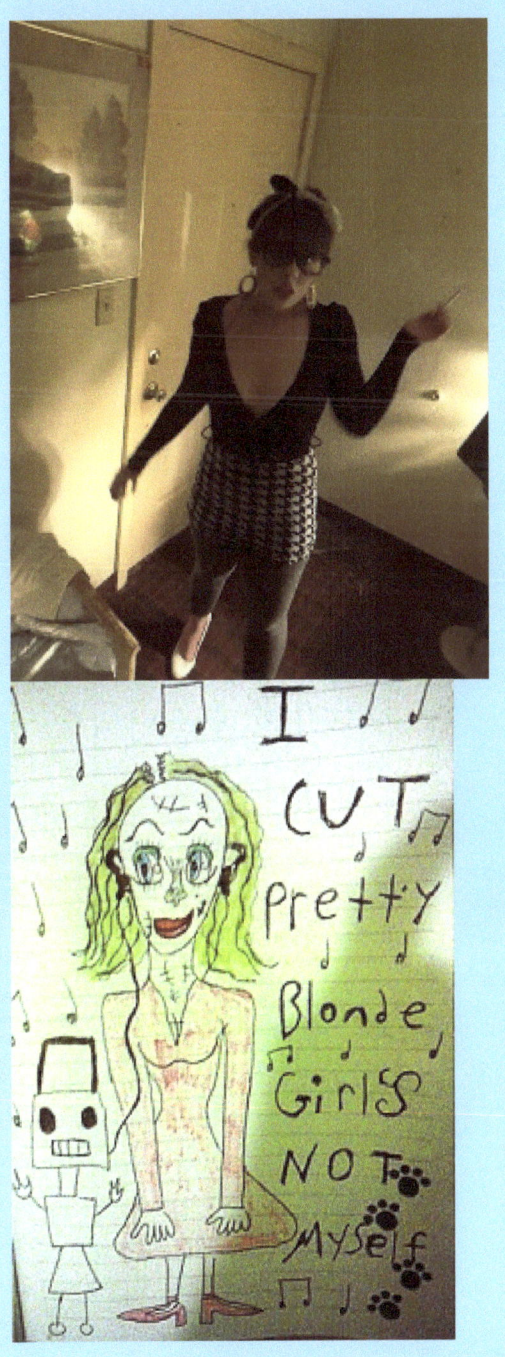

Suicide

In Heaven I'll Be Pretty For Once I Won't Have To Be The Dunce In Heaven Your Vodka Bottle's Always Full Everyone's Equal Everyone's Cool In Heaven You Can Shoot H You Can Shoot Crank No One's Gonna Lock You Up & Call You A Skank In Heaven There's A Boy Who Sings & Plays Sad Guitar He Has Hair Redder Than The Blood I Used To Write These Letters & Eyeshadow Bluer Than My Soul In Heaven There's A Unicorn & You Never Feel Forlorn In Heaven I'm Gonna Need An Eyepatch To Protect Myself From Darts

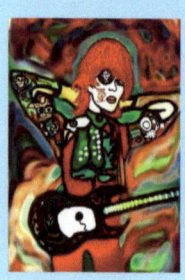

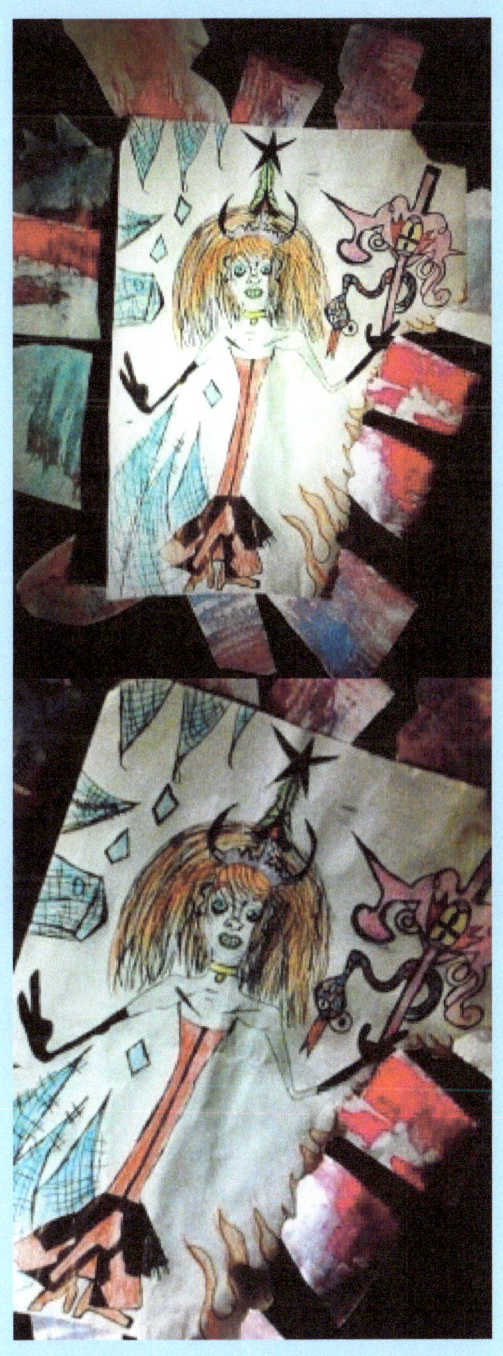

The Ronsequences Of Art

Art Is A Lot Like Driving The More Drugs & Alcohol The Better You Are At It

If Ron Jeremy Goes On Another Crack Cocaine Binge & Buys A Pet Giraffe He Will Have To Pay The Ronsequences Of His Wrong Doing

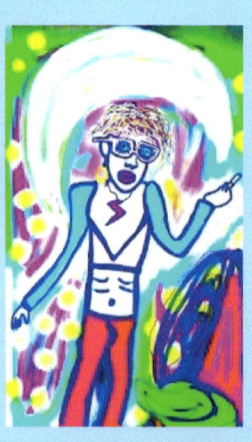

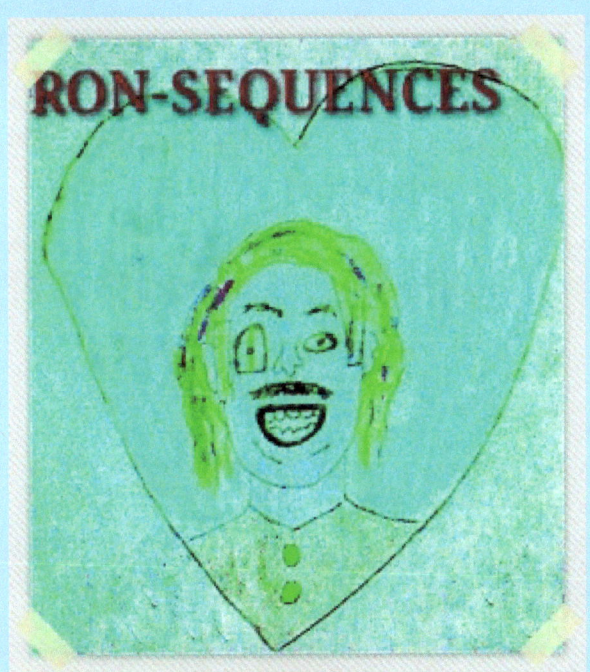
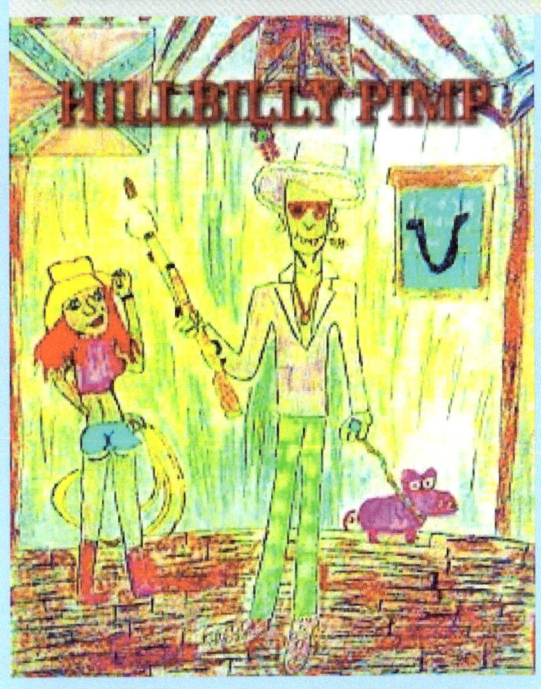

They Told Me To Picture Everyone Naked

And I Got A Boner & The Audience Threw Tomatoes At Me

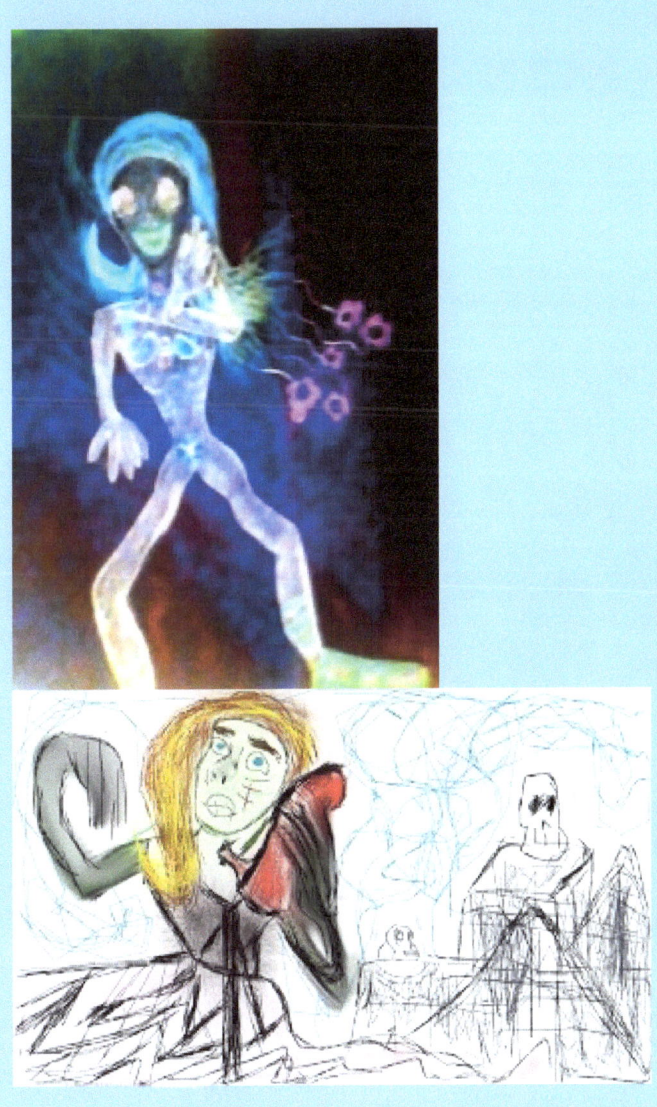

TRAM'S A DOLL

Trams's A Doll Vodoo Sewing Pins Eyes Popping Pinned Out On Tramadol Tram's Your Doll For a Dollar Congratulations Sweaty Slouching 56th Caller Chains Whips & A Spiked Choking Collar

Tramadol, Risperdal, Tylenol, She's On It All Adderall & A Pall Mall She's Paul's Doll Downtown Uppers, Righters, Easters, Downers, Anal, Oral, & All Arounders Tonight's Dinner's Chopstick Stir-Fried Flounder Tram's A Doll Vodoo Sewing Pins Eyes Popping Pinned Out On Tramadol, Risperdal, Tylenol, She's Done It All!

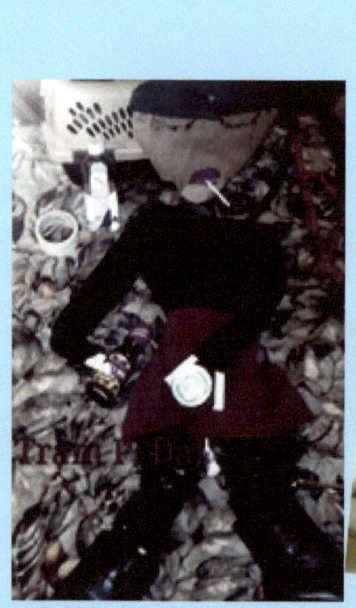
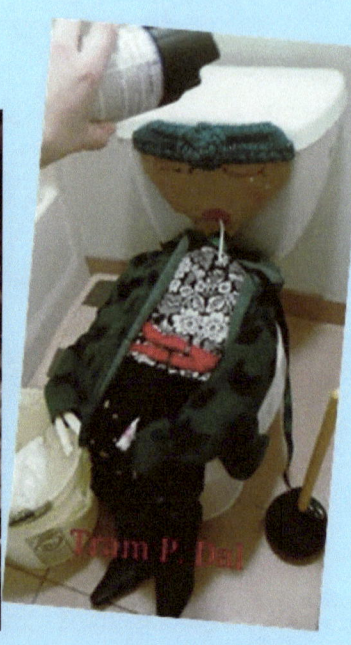

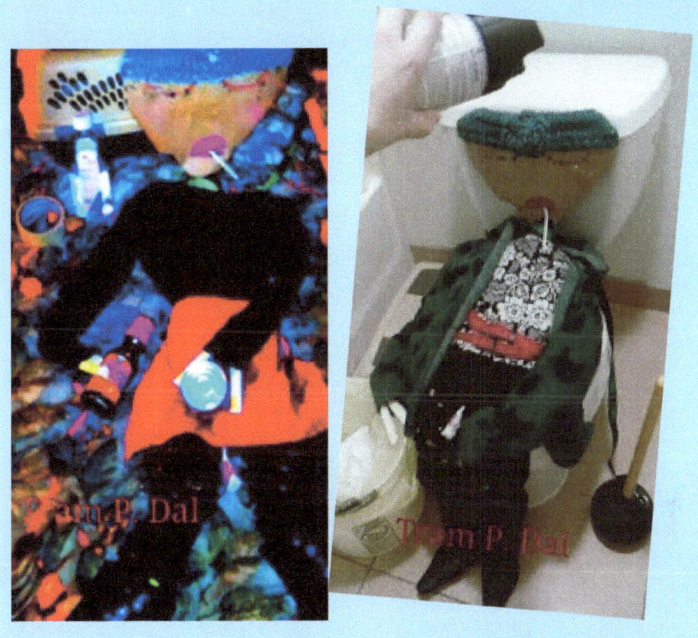

Wino (Morissey Is French For Misery)

I Was Bit By Morrisey As A Young Lad & Now I Suffer From Alcoholism & Depression……..Heaven Knows I'm Morrisey-able Now

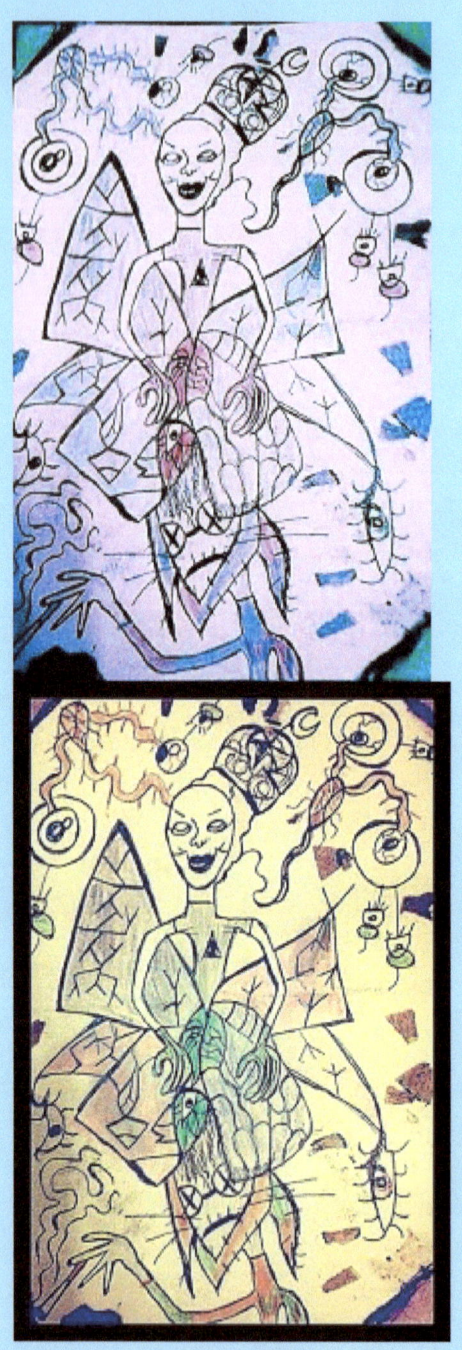

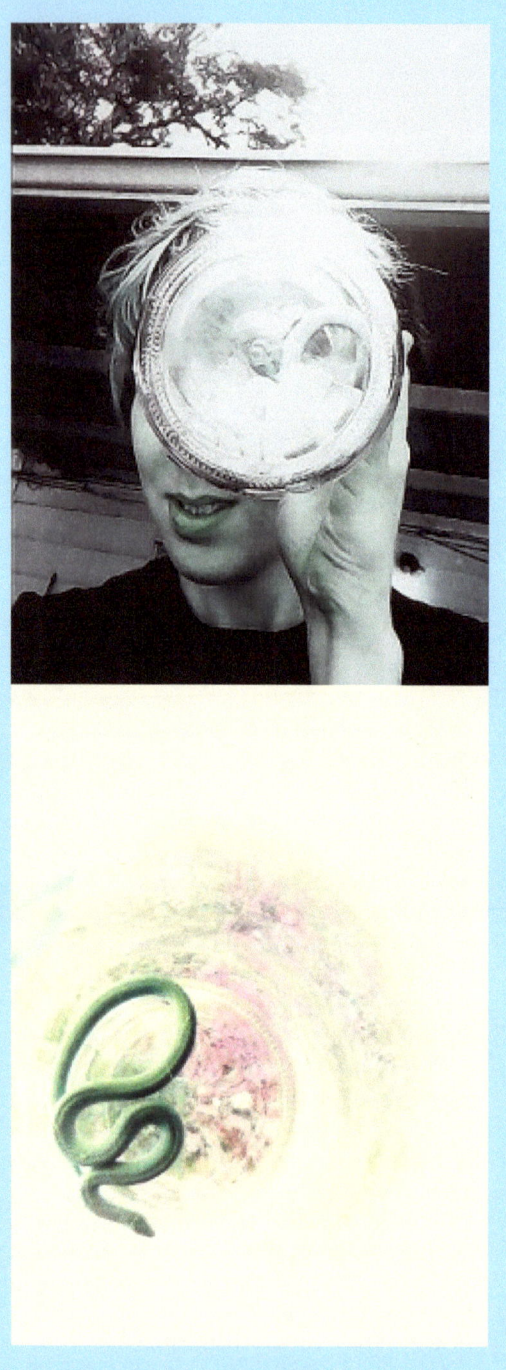

www.ingramcontent.com/pod-product-compliance
Lightning Source LLC
Chambersburg PA
CBHW040325220526
45473CB00009B/2569